Giving the Gift of Encouragement

THE FRAGRANCE OF

KINDNESS

Cheri Fuller

Designed by Left Coast Design Inc. Portland, Oregon.
Printed and bound in Belgium.

ISBN: 08499-5521-1

Published in consultation with the literary agency of

Alive Communications
1465 Kelly Johnson Blvd., Suite 320
Colorado Springs, CO
80920

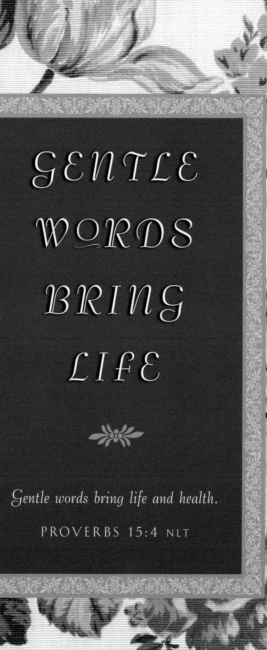

GENTLE WORDS BRING LIFE

❧

Gentle words bring life and health.

PROVERBS 15:4 NLT

Where encouraging words are planted, hope, courage, and confidence grow. Such words dispel discouragement, banish the blues, and bring out the best in people. Gentle words are life-giving; they release potential, light our path, and spur us on to amazing accomplishments. Husbands, children, friends,

Kind words are never wasted. Like scattered seeds, they spring up in unexpected places.

E. M. BOUNDS

and grandparents—people of all ages and stages are desperate for the blessing of encouragement. In fact, they need it as much as plants need water. A miracle can happen when someone is encouraged. As Max Lucado said, "Plant a word of love heart-deep in a person's life. Nurture it with a smile and a prayer, and watch what happens."

*M*any years ago, there were two groups of aspiring writers at the University of Wisconsin who began meeting regularly as a support group. One group named themselves "The Stranglers," and lived up to their name—they critiqued each others' writing abrasively and rarely offered an encouraging word. The other group, "The Wranglers," encouraged all efforts, however feeble. Praise flowed freely in this group and biting words of criticism were never spoken.

Can you ever remember a time when you regretted having said a kind word?

ANONYMOUS

Interestingly, twenty years later, not one person in the critical group had made it as a professional writer. But over half of the encouraging "Wranglers" were successful writers, even nationally known. Among that group was Marjorie Rawlings, author of the award-winning American classic, *The Yearling*.

Everyone has inside of him a piece of
good news. The good news is that you don't
know how great you can be! How much you
can love! What you can accomplish!
And what your potential is!

ANNE FRANK

In praising or loving a child,
We love and praise not that which is,
But that which we hope for.

GOETHE

He was a poor wretch of a little boy who didn't seem to have a chance. His dad was in debtor's prison, he'd only gotten to go to school for four years, and he was often hungry. As a young man he went to work in a rat-infested warehouse putting labels on bottles. He found lodging in a drafty attic room with two other boys from the slums of London.

But he wanted to write. He mailed his first manuscript in the middle of the night so no one would laugh at him, and story after story came back to him, rejected. Finally, when his first story got accepted, he was paid nothing. But the editor praised his work. The young man was so overjoyed he wept. That one bit of encouragement changed his whole life. He wrote with even greater desire and enthusiasm.

Without that editor's few words of praise the young man might have stayed in the dark factories, and the world would have been much poorer for lack of his writing. The boy's name was Charles Dickens.

ENCOURAGING WORDS . . .
LIFT UP THE WEARY

During World War II, China Inland missionary Gladys Aylward was making a harrowing and dangerous journey over the mountains out of war-torn Yangcheng toward free China with more than a hundred orphans in tow. During the desperate days and nights she struggled with despair as never before in her life. After one sleepless night, when she saw utterly no hope of reaching safety and totally felt like giving up, a thirteen-year-old girl in the group reminded her of their beloved story of Moses and the Israelites crossing the Red Sea.

"But I am not Moses!" Gladys cried in desperation.

"Of course you aren't," the young girl said, "but Jehovah is still God!"

Those few hope-filled words from a child infused Gladys with the extra courage she needed to persevere. She and the orphans did make it safely through the mountains to a refuge, proving again God's faithfulness and the power of a person's—even a young person's—words of encouragement and hope.

Far away there in the sunshine are my
highest aspirations. I may not reach
them, but I can look up and see their
beauty, believe in them, and try
to follow where they lead.

LOUISA MAY ALCOTT

A helping word to one in trouble
is often like a switch on a railroad track
. . . An inch between wreck and
smooth, rolling prosperity.

HENRY WARD BEECHER

Every time we encourage someone we
give them a transfusion of courage.

CHUCK SWINDOLL

ENCOURAGING WORDS . . .
GIVE CONFIDENCE

*M*aya walked down the San Francisco hill to take a streetcar to the train station, where she would begin her journey home across the country. Her mother, whom she'd been visiting, accompanied her to the trolley stop. At twenty years old, Maya was struggling to find her way in life but kept running into obstacles and trials. For the past several days, mother and daughter had enjoyed a cherished visit, but now it was time for Maya to return to the fray of everyday life. After kissing her goodbye, Maya's mother said, "You know, baby, I think you're the greatest woman I've ever met."

Her mom turned and slowly made her way up the hill. Maya stood alone, waiting for the streetcar. *Suppose Mom's right*, she thought to herself. *Suppose I really am somebody*. It was a turning point, one of those incredible moments when the heavens roll back and the earth seems to hold its breath. It filled her heart with confidence and hope.

Maya Angelou eventually became a best-selling poet and novelist. She delivered her most famous poem at President Clinton's inauguration.

Drop a stone into the water—
In a moment it's gone,
But there are a hundred ripples
Circling on and on and on—
Say a word of cheer and splendor—
In a moment it is gone
But there are a hundred ripples
Circling on and on.

ANONYMOUS

What ripples can you cause to circle on and on? There are people all around us who desperately need a gentle word of encouragement. Weary single moms, lonely elderly folks, stressed-out teens and others in our churches, neighborhoods, and schools. Write the names of a few people you could encourage this week.

_____

_____

_____

_____

_____

Tommy was in the second grade the year his life intersected with his Aunt Melanie's. His parents had just divorced, and then his dad was shipped to Viet Nam. Tommy's mother was battling mental-health problems and couldn't care for her two boys, so Melanie, a twenty-one year old nurse with no children of her own, and her husband agreed to care for Tommy and James while their mother went into treatment.

You never know when someone may catch a dream from you.

HELEN LOWRIE
MARSHAL

Melanie noticed that Tommy had an interest in subjects related to science. "Tommy, you'd make a wonderful scientist," she encouraged. At Christmas she bought him a microscope, and for his birthday she got him a science testing kit. The following year their dad came home from Viet Nam and took the boys away. He worked as a trucker traveling around the country so the boys were left alone much of the time. When Melanie offered them a home, they said their dad needed them.

As the years passed, Melanie felt regret for not doing more for the boys. When they were in high school their dad left for good. James traveled with him but Tommy was on his own. He worked in a grocery store and lived without running water. But somehow, against all odds, he supported himself, stayed in high school, and managed to put himself through college. Eventually, he was accepted to a top university, where he completed both a master's degree and a doctorate in microbiology.

After graduating from college, Melanie received a letter from her nephew: "I believed in myself because you believed in me," he wrote. "No matter how tough things got in my life I knew I could succeed because you said I could." Today Tommy is a prestigious scientist with a wife and three beautiful children.

Tommy didn't get a lot of things he needed, but apparently during that brief year, he got the thing he needed most: encouragement—the greatest motivator of all.

Make of list of people who encouraged you at the crossroads of your life and helped to point you in the right direction. Recall what they said or did to encourage you. Do you think these individuals realized the impact they had on your life? Perhaps now would be a good time to send them a thank-you note!

_____

_____

_____

_____

_____

_____

_____

_____

_____

_____

_____

If your words have cheered one failing heart
Kindled anew one fading altar fire,
Your work is not a failure;
Chords are touched that will re-echo
from the angel choir.

UNKNOWN

ENCOURAGING WORDS . . .
SHOW LOVE AND SUPPORT

Billy Graham says his mother was one of his greatest encouragers. In his book *Facing Death*, he explained that his mother had always told him to "preach the gospel, and keep it simple." Two weeks before she went to be with the Lord she admonished him with the same words and he responded, "Mother, I'm going to preach His birth, death, and resurrection. I'll preach it till Jesus comes."

There are so many hurts that circumstances and the world inflict upon us, we need the constant reinforcement of encouragement.

BILLY GRAHAM

His mother squeezed his hand and said, "I believe it!"

Having a mother who believed in him and encouraged him meant the world to this man whose life has impacted millions. "What a blessing it is for parents to believe in their children," Graham says.

Judicious praise is to children
what the sun is to flowers.
CHRISTIAN BOVEC

It will take their whole childhood to
complete the job of encouraging [your
children] . . . to go into the world strongly,
as a confident minority, with their heads up.
Tell your children over and over that One
walks with them through all this world's
judgment fires, and that this "one who is
in [them] is greater than the one who
is in the world" (1 John 4:4).
ANNE ORTLUND

Spoken words of encouragement are powerful motivators for children. Words that build up like:

➤ *That's a terrific idea!*

➤ *I'm proud of you! I know you can do it!*

➤ *You are really improving!*

➤ *Thanks for your help.*

➤ *I love you.*

➤ *I really appreciate it when you _____.*

Catch your kids doing something kind, helpful, or responsible, and then give them a picture of what that quality is. Try words like these that give kids a "snapshot" of what they're becoming:

➤ *You are so good at listening patiently and counseling your friends. You could really help hurting people someday.*

➤ *You said you'd feed the dog every day while I was gone, and you did it faithfully. That's what I call responsible!*

➤ *You came up with a solution for that problem I'd have never thought of. What creative thinking!*

When you recognize people's gifts, talents, and areas of effort and improvement, your words acknowledge the best in them. You motivate them to be all God meant them to be.

List here some of the strengths and gifts you could affirm in your spouse, children, friends, or students. Then write a few words of encouragement you could give to each person.

_____

_____

_____

_____

_____

_____

_____

The kindly word that falls today

may bear its fruit tomorrow.

JO PETTY

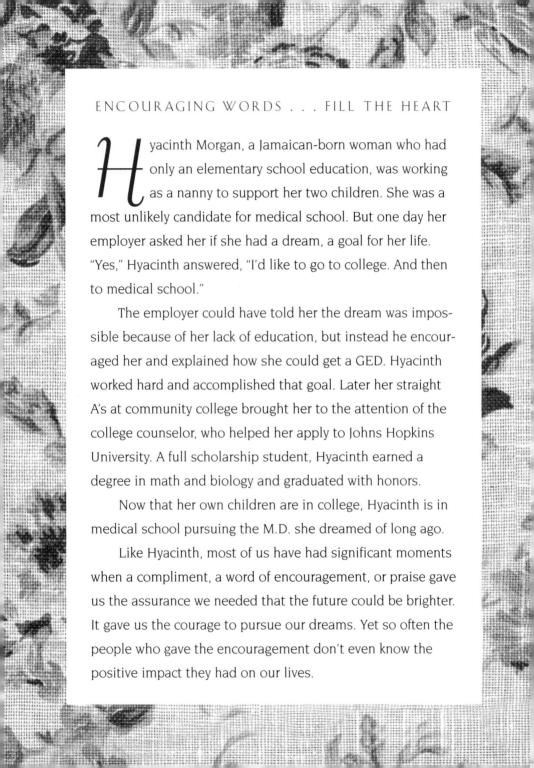

ENCOURAGING WORDS . . . FILL THE HEART

Hyacinth Morgan, a Jamaican-born woman who had only an elementary school education, was working as a nanny to support her two children. She was a most unlikely candidate for medical school. But one day her employer asked her if she had a dream, a goal for her life. "Yes," Hyacinth answered, "I'd like to go to college. And then to medical school."

The employer could have told her the dream was impossible because of her lack of education, but instead he encouraged her and explained how she could get a GED. Hyacinth worked hard and accomplished that goal. Later her straight A's at community college brought her to the attention of the college counselor, who helped her apply to Johns Hopkins University. A full scholarship student, Hyacinth earned a degree in math and biology and graduated with honors.

Now that her own children are in college, Hyacinth is in medical school pursuing the M.D. she dreamed of long ago.

Like Hyacinth, most of us have had significant moments when a compliment, a word of encouragement, or praise gave us the assurance we needed that the future could be brighter. It gave us the courage to pursue our dreams. Yet so often the people who gave the encouragement don't even know the positive impact they had on our lives.

Take with you words, strong words of
courage: Words that have wings! . . .
Tall words, words that reach up,
and growing words, with deep
life within them.

JO PETTY

Encouragement can actually
inflate a deflated attitude because
it fills us with hope.

BARBARA JOHNSON

A little word in kindness spoken,
A motion or a tear,
Has often healed the heart that's broken,
And made a friend sincere.

DANIEL CLEMENT COLESWORTHY

It's your heart, not the dictionary,
that gives meaning to your words.
A good person produces good deeds
and words season after season.

MATTHEW 12:34—35, THE MESSAGE

ENCOURAGING WORDS . . . INSPIRE COURAGE

A young Japanese woman, Atsuko was thrilled with the opportunity to attend college in California. It was a dream come true. But when she arrived on the West Coast, she was overwhelmed with culture shock. She found that people were stressed and harried. Students struggled with their own problems, and no one had time for her. Atsuko felt totally alone.

One of her most difficult classes was volleyball, something that seemed to come naturally to the other students but not to her. One afternoon the instructor told Atsuko to hit the ball to her teammates so they could knock it over the net. Suddenly she froze. Terrified, she feared humiliation if she failed. But a young man on her team somehow understood what she was going through. He walked up to her and whispered, "Come on Atsuko. You can do it!"

"You'll never understand how those words of encouragement made me feel. Four little words: *you can do it*. I felt like crying with happiness." Atsuko was able to knock the ball over the net and made it through volleyball class with flying colors.

Even after returning to Japan and pursuing a career, she never forgot those encouraging words from a classmate. And when things are difficult or seem impossible, she reminds herself of his four simple words: *you can do it*. And she does!

ENCOURAGING WORDS . . .
NOURISH AND ENRICH

*A*fter two years of extensive research with hundreds of men, Patrick Morley (*What Husbands Wish Their Wives Knew About Men*) discovered that men's second greatest need in marriage, besides companionship, is for support. They described this need with words such as "more understanding, support, encouragement, appreciation, respect, affirmation, acceptance, to feel important."

In other words, what husbands are saying is "Help me out here . . . I need some encouragement."

This world is full of people and events that drain faith and spirit from your family, but God has given you the ability to fight off these enemies with loving words of encouragement. Never underestimate their power!

LE ANN WEISS

Here are some encouraging words a wife can say to her husband.
What words would you add to personalize them for your husband?

I love you because _____

_____

Thank you for all you do for our family. Things like _____

_____

I love your (smile or blue eyes or) _____

_____

I appreciate the way you help me by _____

_____

I love the way you love our children, especially when you _____

_____

I admire your strengths. The way you are so (caring, attentive, . . .)

_____

_____

I enjoy being with you. Especially when we _____

_____

_____

TIPS ON ENCOURAGING YOUR HUSBAND:

➤ Avoid criticizing him in front of other people.

➤ Be his most enthusiastic cheerleader.

➤ Affirm your unconditional love, commitment, and acceptance of him.

➤ Extend forgiveness regularly and quickly.

➤ Affirm his positive character qualities and talents.

➤ Pray for him!

If you find yourself becoming critical of your mate, make a list of ten things about him for which you are grateful. Then let him know how much you appreciate these qualities.

We share in God's creative handiwork
when we use words that give life to our
mate's self-esteem. In marriage, one
of the most important things about a
couple is what they say to each other.

BARBARA AND DENNIS RAINEY

Let your speech be always with
grace, seasoned with salt.

COLOSSIANS 4:6

Candy gets stale and flowers wither.
Words and deeds that say "You
enrich my life" go on forever.

LEO BUSCAGLIA

*M*ary Kay Ash is well known for the powerful effect of her encouraging words—not just to large audiences or to the hundreds of "Mary Kay" cosmetics sales representatives she mentors, but even to less visible people, such as the staff in hotel kitchens and the maids cleaning the guest rooms. For years she has stated that God didn't create any nobodies—only somebodies—and everyone has something wonderful about them.

Bless—that's your job, to bless. You'll be a blessing and also get a blessing.

1 PETER 3:7

Whenever she attended a Mary Kay event at a hotel, she insisted on entering through the kitchen. There she would greet workers with a big smile that made them feel important. "Hi! How are you?" she'd say to each person. If they hesitantly responded, "F-f-fine," she'd say, "No, you're great!" Each day, for as long as the event lasted, she was there, repeating her warm greetings.

Hotel managers said she did more for their employees' morale and performance in those few moments than the managers had been able to do in years. Mary Kay's fragrance of kindness was sent out to bless others wherever she went.

ENCOURAGING WORDS . . .
PLANT SEEDS OF GREATNESS

What a powerful impact a grandma's encouraging words can have! When Luciano Pavarotti was a little boy, his grandmother scooped him up into her lap and said, "You're going to be great, you'll see." His mother wanted him to be a banker. But he took a different direction—teaching elementary school, and singing only occasionally. Then his father began to urge him to quit teaching and study music. At age twenty-two, he did. Giving up his teaching position, he became an insurance sales- man so he would have time for voice lessons.

Encouragement through praise is the most effective method of getting people to do their best.

GOTTFRIED R. VON KRONENBERGER

Although Pavarotti credits his father for steering him toward his first love of music, he credits his grandmother as being the source of his inspiration. "No teacher ever told me I would become famous. Just my grandmother."

A kind word is like a Spring day.

RUSSIAN PROVERB

As a professional church soloist, I strive for accurate intonation and pronunciation, good breath-control and projection, and such familiarity with the score that I can sing nearly from memory. But until one life-changing experience, I always thought I fell extremely short of my aspirations.

One Sunday, all professional decorum melted as my high C collided with the organ's piercing C-sharp. Though it was my error, mid-song I had no recourse but to sustain the glaring wrong note.

After the service, Grace, a beautiful, radiant woman, lavished me with undeserved praise. Embarrassed by her compliments, eyes downcast, I lamented, "But Grace, didn't you hear that awful note I caterwauled?"

Without hesitation, she gently encouraged, "Yes, Lynn. But how many *right* notes did you sing?"

I was dumbfounded. How many right notes had I sung? Hundreds? Thousands? With God's grace, my right notes far surpassed the wrong, but I'd never noticed them until her comment.

That one wrong note sung so many Sundays ago, literally changed my life because it fell on Grace's discriminating ears.

LYNN D. MORRISSEY

ENCOURAGING WORDS . . . CHANGE LIVES

A new pastor was called to a country church jokingly called "The Refrigerator" because its parishioners were known for being aloof and unfriendly to visitors and strangers.

When he observed their unfriendliness in action, he didn't criticize or berate them from the pulpit. Instead, whenever he got the chance he talked about them as warm, friendly folks who could have a great impact on their community. Over time, as they listened to his positive descriptions, they gradually took his words to heart and did become kind-hearted, friendly people who attracted new members like never before.

M an's highest duty is to encourage others.

CHUCK SWINDOLL

ENCOURAGING WORDS . . .
BRING OUT THE BEST

She was a shy, quiet girl with long, stringy blond hair. I didn't even know which child she was out of the fifty, noisy fifth-graders I was working with for nine weeks in the "Writer in the Schools" program. I called her name and asked, "Would Brandy come up and read her marvelous poem entitled, 'My Hand'? Students, listen carefully because you're going to love the imagery and word choice in this poem." She walked slowly up to the Author's Chair in our makeshift Reader's Theatre and read her poem aloud to a warm response. "Share some of your other poems," the kids suggested. Slowly, Brandy began to blossom as the class poet.

A few days later I realized how much my few words of encouragement had meant to her when I received this note of thanks:

Dear Mrs. Fuller

These few weeks have been the BEST days of my whole life! YOU brought out the person, the writer inside, that I didn't realize I had. I'll always remember you! And cherish you for what you did for me.

Your ENTHUSIASTIC student, Brandy

LETTERS
MINGLE
SOULS

More than kisses,
letters mingle souls.
JOHN DONNE

*L*etters have the magical capacity to encourage—not once, or twice, but as many times as the recipient pulls out the faded paper the words are written on and rereads them. Even if the stationery has faded and lost some crispness, the thoughts of the heart live on. They renew a sense of being loved and cared about—enough that someone would sit down, put pen to paper, and write the letter.

In our high-tech times of cellular phones and instant e-mail, letter-writing may seem a lost art. Yes, e-mail is handy for keeping in touch with quick notes no matter where you are in the world, but the written note that expresses love or encouragement or praise or a simple hello is a gift from the soul. Whether a scented piece of paper slipped into your husband's briefcase before his business trip, a yellow sticky note tucked into your child's lunchbox, or the simple words "I'm praying for you" on a floral card given to an elderly friend who's been under the weather, notes of kindness have the potential to lift the recipient's spirit, give hope, and fill the heart with encouragement that lasts and lasts.

In a most unique way, written words of encouragement touch other lives with a sweet perfume of kindness.

What cannot letters inspire? They
have souls; they can speak; they have in
them all that force which expresses the
transports of the heart; they have
all the fire of our passions.

HELOISE

A letter always seemed
to me like immortality
Because it is the mind alone
Without corporeal friend.

EMILY DICKINSON

I remember the first letter I received. It was from my great uncle, T. P., who lived in Alaska, which was not yet a state and sounded like a very far-off, fascinating place to a little girl growing up in Texas. He told me what it was like to spend winter in the frozen city of Juneau. He described ice-fishing and tucked in a few photos of Eskimo children who had gone ice-fishing with him. Eskimos and igloos were things I'd seen only in geography books! My uncle's letters opened up a whole  new world of learning for me and provided wonderful writing practice as I responded with letters of my own.

I became hooked on writing letters—and remain so to this day.

A letter can be read and reread. It calms and soothes the sometimes turbulent waters of friendship. A letter, once a part of the writer, now becomes a part of the recipient. Outside of our actual presence, it is the best physical proof we can offer of our friendship, our care and concern for another.
ANONYMOUS

Sit by a crackling fire and read some of your favorite letters. While sitting there soaking up all the love and support, think of one person you love and write a beautiful, loving letter to that person. Let the flame in your hearth warm your heart. One letter in a lifetime to a mother, a daughter, or a special friend could make a greater difference than you dare to believe.
ALEXANDRA STODDARD

*n*ot long ago, my father revealed to me that he still keeps my letter in the top drawer of his desk at home. The pale-blue bond paper is kept safe in its

matching envelope with a flower stamp. He rereads it whenever he feels tempted to smoke a cigarette or when he wants to feel my love for him. A fax would have faded by now. A letter on a floppy disk would be a lot less accessible than one in the top desk drawer. No, my father didn't receive my letter of love and encouragement immediately; it took a few days to arrive through the mail. But today my handwritten letter still speaks to him through the years.

BARBARA L. TYLKA

(*Country Living*, June 1995)

The Fragrance of Kindness

MAKE A WRITING BASKET

I keep a writing basket above my desk for spontaneous notes and letters. When everything's handy in one place, writing a note or letter takes on an ease and enjoyment. Sometimes, just looking at that basket inspires me to dash off a note to a friend or loved one.

If you would like to create a writing basket, let me suggest that you include these items:

- Notecards and envelopes, perhaps imprinted with your name
- Stationery in a variety of colors and textures
- Greeting cards for birthday, get-well, and other occasions
- Thank-you notes
- Stamps
- Favorite pens—in different kinds and colors—calligraphy pen, red pen for Valentine's, Christmas or Fourth of July. (If you have a pen that flows easily, you'll enjoy writing more!)
- Whimsical stickers, stamps and stamp pads for adding personal touches, small Scripture or inspirational cards to tuck into your note.
- Depending on the season, you can include a packet of morning-glory seeds or pressed dried flowers with a delicate scent as an added brightener.

THE TRUE GIFT OF ONESELF

*I*n the mail, buried among mass mailings, catalogues, and Christmas cards was a one-page, single-spaced typed letter. Obviously, it had not been produced on a computer with self-correcting capabilities, but on an old manual typewriter. It was personal . . . to me . . . not a copied Christmas letter. I found this touching. It was from a ninety-two-year-old relative I've never even met. He shared news about the family and his own good health. It was an endearing letter, reminding me of my connections and my talent.

My future and past were rekindled with meaning, wrapped in a simple letter. It made me stop and think about my own gifts to others during the holiday season; it reminded me how precious the gift of self truly is. It put the season in perspective, all in a simple moment of receiving this gift of a letter.

Life is too fast-paced, too commercial, too technical. A true gift is one that touches life's chords, is a true gift of oneself. How simple that a letter can be a gift of time— tucked away, saved, cherished, and passed on.

ANNIE MORTON

LETTERS OF BLESSING

*L*etters become part of our history, and when they are preserved and passed down, they bless the next generations with a glimpse of who they are and where they've been. A letter written by my husband's great-grandmother to her grandson (his grandfather Oliver) shared in just a few sentences a particularly "Fuller" trait of stoicism. Describing the freezing winter of 1905 in Kansas she said, "I don't think we've ever had such a winter here before—lots of snow, deep on the ground . . . then the blizzard. Grandpa had his cap down over his ears and his collar turned up. He looked cold, and the tears were running out of his eyes, but he said he wasn't very cold."

You never know when the words you write today will become a part of tomorrow's history!

A LETTER BOX FOR MOTHER

*D*uring my growing-up years, my mother was a wonderful model of thoughtfulness when it came to sending cards for every occasion. Both she and my father corresponded faithfully with us kids whether we were at camp, college, or, eventually, living a continent away.

However, as Mama entered her seventies, she was prone to forget special occasions, and even when she remembered, had a hard time getting the cards, stamps, address, and mailbox all together at the same time. This gave me the idea for a special Christmas gift for her—one that took a whole year to plan and carry out.

Every holiday that year—Valentine's Day, Mother's Day, Easter—I made a point of buying extra greeting cards and stashing them away for Mama. As Christmas drew close I carefully addressed each card to Mama's extended family (children, grandchildren, sisters, mother) put the proper postage on the envelope and added a sticky note on the front indicating the date it needed to be mailed. Then I placed all the cards in a box, filed them separately by months, wrapped up the box, and gave Mama a whole year's worth of correspondence! All she had to do was sign the card and mail it.

LUCINDA SECREST MCDOWELL

W hen you write a letter to someone, you can encourage dreams, bring cheer, recall fond memories, and re-establish relationships. Here are some people you might want to write:

➤ A faithful friend who has moved away
➤ Your mom or dad, grandparents, aunts, uncles or cousins
➤ Who would you add to your list?

_____

_____

_____

_____

_____

_____

_____

_____

*I*n Thailand, when we went to a camp as coordinators, we designed a small blank notebook for each of the campers with an encouraging verse on the cover. [When you talk, do not say harmful things, but say what people need—words that will help others become stronger. Ephesians 4:29 NCV] During the camp we placed the notebooks on a large central table and encouraged the campers to write positive words, verses, and thoughts on the pages of the other campers' notebooks. On the way home in the bus the campers read their notebooks. I'll never forget the smiles on the Thai campers' faces as they read these affirming words. The teachers were especially gratified as the Thai, who are not verbally expressive with their feelings, were able to show their appreciation of each other through these notebooks.

LARRY DINKINS

LETTERS OF THANKSGIVING

One of the greatest ways to encourage others is to write heartfelt thank-you's for the things they do that bless you, whether a home-cooked meal when you're sick in bed, a thoughtful e-mail note when you're having a bad day at the office, or a gift on your birthday. Leave a paper trail of encouragement in your life to those who help you, work with you, or live with you. The difference between a call and a letter is the difference between the life worth saving and the disposable life. Besides, a letter is the ultimate old-fashioned courtesy between friends, since, unlike the telephone, it never rings and rings, interrupting the flow of life and demanding immediate attention. A letter offers the recipient the luxury of choosing the time and space to add it to her life.

ANONYMOUS

*T*hink back across the years of your life. Can you remember a teacher, mentor, or other person who positively impacted your life? Perhaps a Sunday school teacher, a pastor, or a music professor? Have you ever told that person what a difference they made in your life?

List below a few individuals who come to mind and then purpose to write a note of appreciation today and put it in the mail.

_____

_____

_____

_____

_____

_____

_____

_____

_____

_____

_____

Once Joyce Landorf wrote her pastor a long letter, telling him she'd committed herself to cheering him ever onward. "You preach, I'll turn the pages!" she said in her letter. Later she learned that her letter had arrived during one of the most difficult times of his life when he was about to wither from "pulpit despair" and the same week four disgruntled couples left their tiny sixty-two-member church. Landorf wrote, "Pastor Jim was not touched because my letter was clever or brilliant, but because *God* used the words to bring a healing. But God could not have used an *unwritten* letter."

MAKE THANK-YOU NOTES PART
OF YOUR FAMILY TRADITION

Every year in your child's Christmas stocking and amidst the birthday gifts, include a colorful box of thank-you notes. Then designate a time when your child (or even better, the whole family) will sit down and write a note to each friend and relative who gave a gift.

Gratitude is the memory of the heart.
ANONYMOUS

Even if your child is too young to write, have her dictate a letter of thanks as you write it down. Then illustrate the note with an original picture. You'll be helping your child develop two skills at the same time:

(1) the character quality of gratitude and
(2) creative writing abilities!

If a deed, however humble,
Helps you on your way to go,
Seek the one whose hand has helped you,
Seek him out and tell him so!
UNKNOWN

A SIMPLE NOTE

A few words of encouragement in a simple note written by a teacher on a student's composition or on the manuscript of a fledging writer can make a tremendous difference. That single positive comment can be like a signpost that points the person in the right direction. Notes of hope spur on one's dreams. Words of faith are like a shot in the arm when it is desperately needed.

Who around you deserves or needs a note of approval, affirmation, or encouragement? A vote of confidence or a simple expression of kindness? A simple written note can brighten the receiver's day or motivate him to persevere when things are difficult. It doesn't have to be long. It can even be tacked on to an office report, a student's exam paper, or slipped under someone's coffee cup. Make it short and sincere, and add a specific compliment or word of praise. A few lines not only lift the spirits but can also be kept for other days when a boost is needed. They can even change a life.

> *Let us be grateful to people who make us happy; they are the charming gardeners who make our souls blossom.*
>
> MARCEL PROUST

A LETTER OF BLESSING

Steve Lynn, is a business executive in Nashville. At each milestone in his children's lives, he writes them a letter of blessing such as the one below. It's a precious tradition, and the letters will certainly be treasures for his children to keep forever.

A letter of blessing for Laura Whitney Lynn as she begins middle school:

My dear Whitney,

Our chosen little baby, tomorrow is another major passage as you become a beautiful, unique, young lady. Your Mother and I are grateful for you. We are proud of your external and internal beauty, your bright exploring mind, mothering instincts, loving heart, and creativity.

Through Christ our Lord, I bless you and pray God's blessings upon this step and throughout your life journey. I pray for self-discipline, focus, and commitment to excellence—for balance and enjoyment of the journey—for lots of good friends—and for a focus on relationships rather than things. I encourage you to understand that true freedom comes only from a call to personal responsibility to our fellow man and to our creator.

You have already experienced some of life's hurts. I praise you for how you have overcome them, and I continue to pray daily that you will be surrounded by God's protective angels. You are God's child given to Mom and me for a time until, in a few short years, you are fully ready to be a responsible adult. We are so thankful that you and God chose us. May our Lord bless and keep you.

Love, Dad

People often ask me, "Who encouraged you to be a writer?" When I began writing, there was little career counseling for girls. We were told we could be nurses, teachers, or secretaries, but no one included being a writer. Yet my high-school English teacher, Miss Carpenter, wrote "lucid writing" on my Anna Karenina critical essay and "insightful, articulate thoughts" on my research paper. Her sprinkling of encouraging words on these and other compositions planted seeds of possibility in me, for which I'll always be grateful.

When I began teaching right out of college, I wrote up a list of "99 Ways to Say 'Very Good!'" and kept it right in my grade book, as a reminder to find something positive in every composition or essay I graded for my ninth-grade students. It helped me to encourage them—and thus pass on the kindness I had received.

The purpose of writing inspirational notes is to build others up because there are too many people in the demolition business today.

NORMAN VINCENT PEALE

*f*or years, Clara Ruffin, a middle-school teacher in Connecticut, has written poems to her students' parents. These poems serve a dual purpose of encouraging both the parents and the child for the positive traits she sees in the child. Here's a great example:

> There's a student I call Sunshine
> Who radiates a glow.
> She's positive and pleasant:
> She's someone that you know!
> I recognize home training.
> I mean, it's evident
> The way she speaks, the way she acts
> Is not by accident.
> So parent, I commend you
> For the great work that you do
> The person I'm describing
> Says her training comes from you!

CLARA RUFFIN

From Esteem: Original Poems that Inspire, Entertain, and Build

CREATIVE WAYS TO ENCOURAGE YOUR FAMILY:

- Tuck notes of encouragement in lunch boxes or brown bags.
- Slip notes in tennis shoes or leave on a pillow to be found at bed time.
- Make a Family Mailbox and put in pieces of paper that family members can use to write notes of encouragement and appreciation to each other.
- Create a writing basket for each child, complete with bright notepaper and envelopes, sticky notes, pen or pencil, stickers, and stamps. Encourage your children to write to friends they meet at camp, cousins, and teachers.
- Notes under the bedroom door: When your child's teenage years arrive, you'll be glad if you've already established a custom of writing notes to one another. Notes slipped under the door, such as "Don't forget to take out the garbage," will probably be better received than nagging. And "I'll be cheering for you in tomorrow's soccer game" inspires confidence. Notes such as "I'm sorry I lost my cool last night. Please forgive the spill-over of my stress on you, honey!" are great for apologies and can smooth relationships between parents and teens.

A MESSAGE OF LOVE

Unexpected messages that say "I'm thinking of you when we're apart" speak volumes. Preparing a sandwich for his lunch one day, Mike, a Texas minister, discovered a slip of paper tucked between the slices of bread. "I love you," his wife, Suanne, had written. Several days later, Suanne found an elaborately wrapped surprise on the front seat of her car as she set off for work. Laughing with  delight, she found a package of her favorite Oreo cookies under all the pretty wrappings. What simple and inexpensive ways to say "I love you"!

A LETTER IN THE SKY

fter former President Richard Nixon resigned from the presidency in shame and humiliation, he had to undergo major surgery. Overwhelmed with so much disappointment and physical pain, Nixon became severely depressed. Lying in the hospital room day after day, he began to lose hope and even the will to live. He told his wife Pat that he wanted to die. But at his lowest moment, a nurse came into the room, opened the curtains, and pointed to a small plane flying back and forth in front of his window. It was pulling a sign that read: "GOD LOVES YOU AND SO DO WE!"

An anxious heart weighs a man down, but a kind word cheers him up.

PROVERBS 12:25

Seeing that letter written across the sky, and sensing the loving prayers behind it gave Nixon the courage to recover. Later, he found out that Ruth Bell Graham had personally arranged for the plane to fly around the hospital. The former president not only survived, but went on to serve both his family and country with dignity and grace for several years.

What strength comes with positive words of encouragement—whether spoken or written across the sky!

If instead of a jewel, or even a flower,
We could cast the gift of a lovely
thought into the heart of another,
That would be giving as
the angels must give.
GEORGE MACDONALD

EXCHANGING LOVE LETTERS

arriage Encounter weekends have helped thousands of couples recover the lost art of writing love letters, communicating with each other, and learning to share personal feelings in a heart-to-heart encounter. Here's how you can incorporate this idea in your marriage. First determine a question you both want to answer like, "What qualities do I love most about you?" (or a question related to children, work, or anything else). Spend 5-10 minutes writing an answer to the question and expressing your feelings in loving detail. After exchanging letters, talk about your responses. Reach out to understand your spouse's feelings. Write these "love letters" weekly or more often and watch your relationship grow.

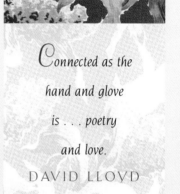

Connected as the

hand and glove

is . . . poetry

and love.

DAVID LLOYD

ANNIVERSARY POEMS

*f*or nearly every anniversary of out thirty-year marriage, I have written a poem to my husband, Holmes, and presented it to him as a gift. It serves as a reminder of how our relationship has grown and how grateful I am for him, along with my hopes for our future. Each year as he reads the poem, whether by candlelight or

in the harsh glare of a MacDonald's restaurant (once when we were moving back to Oklahoma from Maine), his heart is encouraged and warmed.

The Fragrance of Kindness

MY ANNIVERSARY POEM—XXVI

We married on an autumn Saturday
twenty-six years ago,
but it was the spring of our marriage.
Texas weather was sunny, our outlook as bright
as the yellow mums blooming all around the church.
We drove away in a white Chevy Nova
as family and friends smiled and cheered
to an overnight stay, then back to Waco
where our jobs and reality awaited.
As we joined our lives and hearts, our destinies,
God's grace was always near the third strand of our
    relationship.
So in seasons to come, during the winters of our marriage—
some more joyful and painful
than we'd ever dreamed—
we would stand
and stand together.

May our hearts
keep dancing always,
celebrating the gift of life
all our days.

MUCH LOVE, CHERI

*D*uring the nine months of pregnancy, there are so many special moments to remember. Why not write your loving thoughts in letters to your unborn child? You might want to put all the letters in a journal to give to your child someday as a source of encouragement and a lifelong treasure.

If you want to extend the life of the journal, you can continue to write keepsake notes as your child grows. Write about things you're proud of, family history you want to pass on, and your gratefulness for all the chances your child gives you to go to the park, make sandcastles at the beach, make birthday cakes, and give fun parties!

(sample notes for baby's journal)

April 26, 8 weeks in utero

> Dear Baby,
>
> Your daddy and I were totally amazed when we saw your first picture on the ultrasound. We could also hear your heart beating so fast! It was incredible! Daddy carries your "picture" with him all the time, and mine is on the refrigerator. Friends and family who have seen your first picture have fallen in love with you just as we have. Your daddy thinks you're going to be very smart since your head is so big!
>
> Totally in awe, Mommy

August 10, 24 weeks in utero

Dear Active One,

I finally felt you kick and move for the first time! Your mommy has felt you for a while and I've been jealous! I was relaxing in front of the TV tonight when mommy said, "Come here!" She placed my hand firmly on her stomach, and I waited. Suddenly, you pushed against my palm. I smiled so big. We both laughed. Then you did it again, and again. Boy, can you move! We spend a lot of time watching and feeling and dreaming about you. We can't wait to hold you!

Daddy

September 4, 28 weeks in utero

Dear Baby,

I love being pregnant with you and feeling you move. What a blessing God has bestowed on moms! It's nice to know you are always with me. People keep reminding me to enjoy this season when you're so easy to tote around, because once you arrive, we'll have to take along a bunch of stuff for you. Your daddy and I don't care; we just want to cuddle with you and hug you and kiss you.

You are so loved, Mommy

SOME CREATIVE LETTER WRITING TIPS:

➤ When you travel, carry a small fabric portfolio or letter folder with you. Inside, tuck: stamped postcards, notepaper, and envelopes. Include extra stamps for scenic postcards you find along your journey. In only a few minutes you can write a highlight of your travel day or share an encouraging word on the postcard and pop it in a mailbox.

➤ When you give a gift, include a note expressing your affection or friendship. Books with personal notes written on the inside cover are special blessings to the recipient!

➤ Write a letter or send a postcard to a child you know, whether your grandchild in town or a young friend far away, and encourage the child to write back to you. Tuck in a humorous comic strip, a stick of gum, or a magazine article about something he's interested in. You may just be the catalyst to start this fortunate young person on a lifetime habit of writing letters.

➤ Keep stamped postcards in your Bible. When someone comes to mind in your quiet time and you pray for them, write a few lines to let them know and drop it in the mail.

GRACIOUS GIFTS—ALWAYS IN GOOD TASTE

❋

The only true gift is
a portion of yourself.

RALPH WALDO EMERSON

Whether the gift is handmade or thoughtfully chosen at a store, from your garden or kitchen, quilted or painted, from across the world or right from your own backyard—gifts given in a spirit of love and kindness can deliver buckets of encouragement to the recipient. The time and care it takes to give a gracious, personal gift speaks volumes—and gives pleasure both to the giver and receiver. A steaming pot of chicken soup delivered to a friend's door when she's had surgery encourages her to "Get well soon!" A gift of fragrant flowers can say "I love you" or "I'm sorry" or "You did a great job!" Handmade quilts and crafts convey friendship; gift baskets can be personalized to meet the needs of someone we love.

There are expected gifts given at holidays or birthdays, but the spontaneous, unexpected gift from the heart is perhaps best of all. To give gracious gifts, we can think, "What would make this person happy or lighten her load?" "What does she need today?" or "What would bring delight?" Whatever the answer to that question, in the process of giving and receiving gracious gifts, kindness blossoms!

GIFT-TAG IDEAS

When you give a gift, add the blessing of God's Word on a specially written tag:

➤ For a gift of athletic shoes: *"I will run the course of Your commandments, for You shall enlarge my heart"* (Ps. 119:32).

➤ For baby bath items in a tote: *"Live clean, innocent lives as children of God"* (Phil. 2:15b)

➤ A box decorated like a book and filled with goodies for a favorite school student: *"Happy is the man who finds wisdom, and the man who gains wisdom"* (Prov. 3:13)

➤ A handmade comforter or afgan: *"Blessed be the God and Father of our Lord Jesus Christ, the Father of mercies and God of all comfort, who comforts us in all our tribulation."* (2 Cor. 1:3)

CAROL CUTLER

*M*y dear friend Mary began quilting several years ago. Giving her handmade quilts away as gifts is a joy to her and to those who receive them. When each of her nieces and nephews had a baby, Mary designed and made them a crib quilt. For friends who were getting married, she created a wedding quilt. But how

*I*nto my quilts I stitch the memory of our friendship.

ROXY L. BURGARD

delighted I was when our first grandbaby was born and I received the beautiful white, purple, and red "Grandma Quilt" that Mary had carefully stitched. In a block at the top it said, "Grandchildren are the gifts of yesterday, the pride of today, and the joy of tomorrow. Celebrating the grandchildren of Holmes and Cheri Heath Fuller . . . Quilted with love from your childhood friend, Mary Jaynes Mayer, April 23, 1998." In one block she wrote our granddaughter's birth date and weight, and saved the other blocks for grandchildren to come. What fun to have this precious gift of love to cuddle around our grandchildren when they come to our house.

STITCHED WITH LOVE

*I*n the nineteenth century, friendship quilts were popular gifts. When young women moved westward during the expansion of America, they took their friendship quilts with them and, in a sense, the love of friends and family who had stitched the colors and fabrics together.

Once again, friendship quilts are flourishing today. In Lucinda McDowell's book *Quilts from Heaven*, she tells how she made her first friendship quilt as a wedding gift to her younger sister, Susan. Eight months before the wedding, Cindy sent each of Susan and her fiancè, Glen's, friends and family members a 10-inch square of muslin along with an invitation to participate in making the quilt. They could use any colors and any

*O*ne who sleeps under a
quilt is comforted by love.
UNKNOWN

style to create a square that represented their relationship to the bride and groom, and somewhere in their square they were to place their name and a heart. By winter, fifty-six completed squares had arrived in the mail, so the quilting began. Love went into every stitch as she prayed for the marriage that would be built on God's love. Displayed at the wedding reception, Susan and Glen's quilt continues to grace their bed, just as twenty-one years later, they continue to live in the power of God's faithfulness and love. One day their quilt will be a precious legacy to pass on to their daughters.

LUCINDA SECREST MCDOWELL

THE GIFT OF COMPASSION

One day last summer, hiking with two of the children through the hills of north Georgia, I came to a tiny cabin clinging to a rocky ledge. Behind a picket fence a white-haired mountain woman was working in her garden. When we stopped to admire her flowers, she told us that she lived there all alone. My city-bred youngsters regarded her with wonder. "How," asked one, "do you keep from being lonesome?" "Oh," she said, "if that feeling starts to come on in the summertime, I take a bunch of flowers to some shut-in. And if it's winter, I just go out and feed the birds!" An act of compassion—that was her instinctive antidote for loneliness. And it made her immune.

> *How far that little candle throws his beams! So shines a good deed in a naughty world!*
>
> WILLIAM SHAKESPEARE

ARTHUR GORDON

A Touch of Wonder

GIFTS FROM THE KITCHEN

Homemade food is a gift from the heart. The fragrance of kindness that accompanies homemade bread, cinnamon rolls, or even a simple cocoa mix in a bright mug delivers much comfort and encouragement. Whether you are rejoicing over a friend's new baby, giving relief to someone who is ill, or welcoming new neighbors, gracious giving from the kitchen doesn't have to be complicated. When you bake muffins, fix an extra batch and freeze it for spontaneous giving. When you make a casserole, divide it in half and give some to a shut-in who would love a home-cooked

meal. You will leave someone feeling a little merrier and maybe make a new friend.

GRANDMA'S SIMPLE GIFT

Throughout her eighty-eight years of life, my great grandma Flossie Jenkins greeted her new neighbors with freshly baked cinnamon rolls. If anyone moved within three blocks of her home, she'd walk her petite 4'8" self down the road to greet them with a smile, some friendly chatter, and her famous rolls. Fortunately, she passed her generous spirit and recipe on to her daughter, my grandma.

It's loving and giving that makes life worth living.
UNKNOWN

I can never bake or eat a cinnamon roll without seeing grandma in her red-checkered apron mixing, kneading, and rolling out dough. With an unexplained peacefulness, I'm transformed to a little girl perched on the oak stool, ready to assist. With infinite patience, my grandma taught me the finer points of making cinnamon rolls. She created a beautiful memory and legacy —one I've passed on to my own child.

SHENAE NICHOLSON

GRANDMA FLOSSIE'S CINNAMON ROLLS

Soak 1 cake yeast in 1/4 cup lukewarm water and set aside
Beat 1 egg and set aside

In mixing bowl, combine:

> 1/4 cup butter
>
> 1/4 cup sugar
>
> 1 1/4 tsp. salt
>
> 1 cup boiling water

Cool mixture, then stir in 1 cup flour. Add yeast and egg and 2 1/2 cups of flour.

Roll out dough in a 1/3 inch thick rectangular shape. Spread melted butter on top and sprinkle with cinnamon and sugar. Roll up lengthwise as tightly as possible. Slice and place in a cake pan that has been rubbed with butter. Let rise until double.

Bake in a 350 degree oven for 15-20 minutes or until golden brown on top.

Remove from oven. While still warm frost with icing: mix 1/4 cup butter, 2 cups powdered sugar, 1 teaspoon vanilla, and drops of milk to desired consistency. Mix over low heat until smooth.

These rolls are wonderful for family brunches, for wrapping with cellophane and ribbons and giving to a new family on the block or to someone who's been ill and needs cheering up!

She who gives is twice blessed.

UNKNOWN

The gift is small

But love is all.

UNKNOWN

The Fragrance of Kindness

A MUG TO WARM THE HEART

*T*his gift is sure to please your child's teacher or a friend on any fall or winter day. Add a little card or gift-tag that says, "Thanks for being a forever friend" or "A teacher affects eternity—she can never tell where her influence stops."

Mix:

The Lord loves a cheerful giver.

2 CORINTHIANS
9:7

> 3 1/2 cups brown sugar, packed
>
> 2 cups cocoa
>
> 2 teaspoons ground cinnamon
>
> 1/2 teaspoon ground nutmeg
>
> 1/4 teaspoon salt

Blend well in a blender or bowl, and store in an airtight container, ready to give away. Put some of the mix in a baggie, tied with a bright ribbon. Place this in a cup along with some marshmallows. Wrap the cup in some bright cellophane.

Include these instructions on a gift tag: *Stir 1 1/2 tablespoons of the mix into 6 ounces of hot milk, top with marshmallows and enjoy!*

THE SWEET TASTE OF KINDNESS

*I*t's helpful to have at least one foolproof recipe that always turns out well, so you feel good about giving it away. Then, when there's a need among friends or family, it's easy to whip something up that spells and tastes "LOVE." For some, that may be cookies, a cake, or even enchiladas. My personal favorite is *Susan's Banana Bread,* named for my friend Susan Payson, who never throws out an overripe banana. I've given loaves of banana bread as Christmas gifts, get-well gifts, and "thinking of you" gifts. I've given them to elderly friends and a widowed pastor.

Banana bread is delicious, warmed for breakfast or afternoon tea. On the following page you will find an easy recipe that turns out two delicious loaves of banana bread—one to keep and one to give away!

SUSAN'S BANANA BREAD

3 bananas

1 egg

1 cup sugar

3 tablespoons melted butter

2 cups flour

1 teaspoon each baking soda and baking powder

1/2 teaspoon salt

Mash, mix, and pour into two medium-size loaf pans that have been lightly greased. Bake at 350 degrees for 45 minutes, or until a toothpick inserted in the middle of the loaf comes out clean.

Cool loafs, remove from pan and wrap in clear wrap. To keep them fresh overnight, refrigerate.

Not what we give,
But what we share,
For the gift without
the giver is bare.

JAMES
RUSSELL
LOWELL

THE GIFT OF A PICNIC

*M*aureen, a young mother with two little ones, and her husband were struggling financially. It seemed they were so busy scrimping and "getting by" that life was just passing them by. They often felt discouraged and depressed. Then one Sunday someone in their church delivered the kindest gift they had ever received. An older couple called and told Maureen not to worry about fixing lunch on Sunday. She thought they were going to invite her little family over to eat or take them to a restaurant. Instead, after the final hymn was sung and the congregation dismissed, the elderly couple handed Maureen a colorful blanket, a full picnic basket, and a map with directions to an unknown destination.

Maureen and her family followed the map to a wildflower meadow ablaze with color: red poppies, yellow coreopsis, purple irises, wild daises, and all kinds of native flora. There, amidst the beauty of a spring meadow, they relaxed and enjoyed the delicious picnic lunch. The children dipped their feet in the clear pond as Maureen delighted in the butterflies and singing birds. Her heart was deeply touched by this kind act. Somehow her burdens felt lighter.

For many years after that Sunday, the family returned to the wildflower meadow—a fragrant reminder of the gift of kindness.

MAKE A PICNIC BASKET

A picnic can turn an ordinary afternoon into a time for romance for a couple or spontaneous fun for kids and parents. Whether you make a picnic basket for a needy family or surprise your own family and friends, here's how to get ready:

- Set aside a large wicker basket (a fruit or flower basket will do).
- Stock it with festive paper plates, napkins, and plastic forks and knives.
- Add a jar of cold lemonade, turkey or tuna sandwiches, chips, fruit, cookies, or other favorite family foods. (If you are planning a romantic picnic, you might adjust the menu to include French cheeses, a loaf of fresh bread, and other favorite delicacies.)
- Tuck in a frisbee, a checkered tablecloth, and a blanket to sit on.
- Set off for a nearby park or lake, and give your family the gift of a happy memory!

> *You never know when you're making a memory.*
> RICKIE LEE JONES

BASKETS OF KINDNESS

With very little effort, a gift basket can be tailor-made for people who need a little encouragement: a new family in the neighborhood, a friend who's been ill, or someone who simply needs some tender-loving care.

Gift baskets are appropriate at any season of the year. At Thanksgiving you can fill a large basket with food for a needy family. At Christmas you can fill small baskets with gingerbread treats for neighborhood children. In the spring or summer, why not give away a basket brimming with flowers?

A basket can serve a practical need when you fill it with gardener's tools and a pair of gloves for your favorite friend. Chock-full of fresh fruit and trail mixes, a basket is a perfect gift for college students studying for finals.

A gift basket is a fun and practical way to deliver kindness and encouragement when they are needed most.

A WELCOMING BASKET

*M*oving is not only exhausting, it's often a lonely experience, especially for those who move into a community where they have no friends. When you see a new family unpacking the moving van, why not put together a welcome basket of healthy snacks and finger foods. Add a tag that says, "Welcome to Our Neighborhood!" and perhaps a map of the area or other helpful information. You'll start off on the right foot, encouraging your new neighbors when they need it the most—in the midst of putting down new roots.

That best portion of a good [woman's] life: Her little, nameless, unremembered acts of kindness and of love.

WILLIAM WORDSWORTH

A VALENTINE BASKET

Just as Valentine's day was approaching, Justin and Tiffany, our son and daughter-in-law, had to spend long days in the neonatal intensive care unit where their new baby was critically ill. Chris and Magie, our second son and his fiancèe, wanted to cheer up the anxious parents so they prepared a beautiful white basket, bedecked

When I give, I give myself.

WALT WHITMAN

with a red bow. Inside the basket they placed a container of chicken Caesar salad, some Italian bread, several Valentine chocolates, a bottle of sparkling cider, handy disposable wine glasses and dishes, and a lovely tablecloth. This thoughtful gift, delivered to a lonely waiting room on an otherwise dreary night, brought a much needed boost of encouragement and gave two young hearts a few romantic moments together in the midst of a trying time.

GIFT BASKETS TO CHEER
THE BODY AND SOUL

➤ Place your favorite soup or chili in a jar in a basket. Add some herb-seasoned bread, several pieces of fruit, and a pretty cloth napkin. Deliver to a shut-in or a lonely single person.

➤ Make a movie night basket with microwave popcorn, a video movie, and soda pop in cans. This is sure to cheer a friend when all her children are homebound with the flu or a busy teacher with papers stacked to the ceiling. Include a gift tag that says: "A cheering-up for you!"

Surely great lovingkindness yet may go
With a little gift: all's dear that comes from friends.
THEOCRITIS

It is more blessed to give than to receive.
ACTS 20:35

GIFTS FROM YOUR GARDEN

Some of the best gifts are those created from the bounty of your garden, whether a simple basket filled with cut flowers from backyard blooms, lavender sachets made from an herb garden, or a rosebud from a local florist. Flowers speak a language all their own and carry an unmistakable fragrance of kindness.

By chivalries as tiny
A blossom, or a book,
The seeds of smiles are planted
Which blossom in the dark.

EMILY DICKINSON

One is nearer God's heart in a garden
than anywhere else on earth.

DOROTHY FRANCES GURNEY

BOUQUETS OF KINDNESS

*P*lant a garden of wildflowers or others flowers ideal for cutting—daisies, bachelor buttons, buttercups, hollyhocks, and corn flowers or sweetbriar. Don't just fill your own vases with blooms but grow enough to share with a friend or neighbor. Arrange any spring or summer blooms in a simple bouquet. Wrap a bright ribbon around the stems, include a gift card that says, "If God cares so wonderfully for flowers that are here today and gone tomorrow, won't He more surely care for you" (Matt. 6:30), and watch the smiles grow!

Happiness is the art of making a bouquet of those flowers within reach.

PISSARO

GARDEN GIFT-TAG IDEAS

➤ Give a tote or basket with garden tools and accessories and add a gift tag with this verse: "*Let your roots grow down into Him and draw up nourishment from Him. See that you go on growing in the Lord, and become strong and vigorous in the truth you were taught*" (Col. 2:7).

➤ On a gift tag to accompany homemade jam from the fruits of your garden write this verse: "*The fruit of the Spirit is love, joy, peace, patience, kindness, generosity, faithfulness, gentleness and self-control*" (Gal. 5:22).

➤ How about this verse on a gift tag with a green plant: "*He who trusts in His riches will fall, but the righteous will flourish like the green leaf*" (Prov. 11:28).

GIVE A GIFT OF LAVENDER

My mother-in-law grows lavender in her garden. It's easy to grow and when dried and placed in a delicate muslin bag makes a wonderfully fragrant gift.

You'll need muslin bags, satin ribbon, dried lavender heads, and tiny silk flowers. (Inexpensive muslin tea bags can be purchased at a health food store.)

Fill each bag with dried lavender flowers. If desired, add a few miniature silk flowers for extra color. Tie each bag with a satin ribbon and give this lovely gift to say "thank you" or to let someone know they are as special as the lovely fragrance of lavender. This is a gift that will keep on giving for months and months.

Note: If you don't grow lavender, you can purchase dried lavender in hobby or craft stores or through wholesale florists. All other items can be purchased at hobby, craft, or fabric stores.

ROSE—PETAL SACHETS

I love all kinds and colors of roses: tropicana, elegant crimson, yellow... and white, climbing roses, old roses, country cottage roses. I find rose petals carry a special fragrance of kindness, even after the blooms have faded from their original glory. One of the oldest recorded garden gifts (dating back to the Roman Empire), rose petals

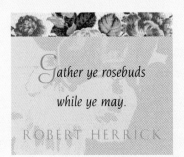

Gather ye rosebuds while ye may.

ROBERT HERRICK

make wonderful fresheners for a closet or lingerie drawer. In years gone by, rose petals were thought to cheer the heart.

It's easy to make a rose-petal sachet. Simply mix:

3 ounces rose petals

1 teaspoon ground orris root

25 drops rose essential oil

Fill small fabric or muslin bags with this mixture, tie with a satin ribbon, and gift as a surprise gift to a friend!

Note: The orris root and essential oil can be purchased at a hobby shop, or herb, garden, or health food store. If you don't grow your own roses, you can get rose petals from the discard piles at local grocery store florists or floral shops. Call ahead and ask if they will save the discarded petals for you.

ROSE PETAL BODY SPRAY

This is another great gift idea that is simple to make and such fun to give!

Just bring 1 cup of pink or red rose petals and 1 cup of water to a boil. Let the mixture boil for a minute. Cover the pan and let the liquid cool. Strain the liquid through a colander or sieve and pour it into a pretty spray bottle. Refrigerate to keep fresh until you are ready to give it away. (The spray will keep indefinitely in the refrigerator, but only a week if it is not refrigerated.)

If I can put one touch of rosy sunset into the life of any man or woman, I shall feel that I have worked with God.

GEORGE MACDONALD

When we were loading the moving van in Akron, Steve called up the stairs, "Dee, you have a visitor!" I was surprised to find Phyllis, a woman from my Bible study, perched quietly on a big box in the living room. Phyllis had never been to see me before. My surprise grew as she silently held out a beautiful afghan. For months she had been spending evenings crocheting this expression of love. Phyllis, undisputedly the most reserved member of  all the women in the study, loved me! Spontaneously, I hugged her. At first her arms hung limply at her sides, but then she returned my embrace. Unwiped tears ran down our cheeks and my heart was encouraged for yet another move.

DEE BRESTIN
The Friendships of Women

*Those who bring sunshine to the lives
of others cannot keep it from themselves.*

JAMES BARRIE

*One of the deep secrets of life is
that all that is really worth doing
is what we do for others.*

LEWIS CARROLL

WILD STRAWBERRIES FROM RUSSIA

*D*eep in the woods of central Russia, wild strawberries have thrived through the vaults of centuries. These tiny berries and their hearty runners have stretched through years of tsars, invaders, and wars. Instinctively, small grandmas—*babas*—knew just how to transplant them into their gardens. In 1987, when the Cold War still existed, one such *baba*, my longtime pen pal, Anastasia, lived inside a little dacha in the outskirts of Vladimir. One day she sat down and wrote a letter explaining how to plant wild strawberry seeds in a pot, where to place them in the house, and how to water and transfer the sprouts from a windowsill to the garden.

Across nine time zones and thousands of air miles, Anastasia's letter arrived at my house in St. Louis, Missouri, late one September afternoon. Like so many previous letters, it came in an inexpensive, pale envelope, worn at the edges and frayed at the corners. When I opened it, I was surprised to find a tissue paper folded inside. And even more amazed to find that the tissue paper held countless tiny seeds—wild strawberry seeds from Russia. The treasured seeds had passed through postal hands, bypassed customs, and left their Mother Russia forever. I wondered how these native berries would survive in the foreign soil of mid-America, but decided to put the seeds aside until spring.

Finally, in March, I carried out Anastasia's potting instructions. To my utter amazement, slender seedlings appeared within a week! By July, the seedlings had grown too big to remain in the pot so I planted them in a row along the back fence. Miraculously, they not only endured the alien soil and fierce Missouri heat, but spread out and blossomed profusely—as if to celebrate their survival! By the following spring, they had propagated even further, and yielded a multitude of delicious red berries!

FERN AVERS MORRISSEY

SURPRISE GIFT IDEAS

Your Bible study leader: A Bible commentary or new devotional book with a gift-tag that says, *"Open my eyes to see wonderful things from your Word!"* (Ps. 119:18)

An elderly woman: Put together the ingredients for an instant tea party, with cookies and a little box of lemon tea bags. Add a gift-tag that says, *"May God send you wonderful times of refreshment from being in the presence of the Lord"* (Acts 3:19b). Then stay a while for conversation.

A single mother: Even practical gifts are greatly appreciated. Like a disposable camera with a certificate for developing film.

List some other gift ideas that might come in handy:

_____

_____

_____

_____

_____

_____

_____

A POCKETFUL OF TIME

❃

*Always set a high value
on spontaneous kindness.*

SAMUEL JOHNSON

GIVING THE GIFT OF TIME

Since love is spelled T-I-M-E, giving the gift of time is perhaps one of the kindest gifts of all. When a mom spends uninterrupted time snuggling with her child and reading a book or a teacher listens to her student, love fills the heart of the child. When a wife puts down her work to welcome her husband with a big hug as he comes in the door, he's encouraged and affirmed. When friends meet for lunch and hear what's going on in each other's lives, their hearts are refreshed. When we set aside time to volunteer, visit a shut-in, or offer hospitality to a new family on the block, the angels must surely applaud our encouragement-in-action! In this hurry-up world where time is measured in nanoseconds, making time for people is a challenge—but it's worth the effort. Giving a pocketful of time always encourages, lifts up the heart, and renews the spirit. And in the process of blessing others, we find ourselves refreshed.

She who refreshes others
will herself be refreshed.

PROVERBS 11:25

When God's children are in need,
we can be the ones to help them out—
and the results of our caring can be beyond
measure. We never know at the time whether
we are God's instrument for changing a life.

EMILIE BARNES

DETERMINED TO SHOW LOVE

*I*s there anything I can do?" the eagerness in my friend's voice touched me. Many others had asked my husband and I that question, and I'm sure each of them felt there was little they could do. In just over a year's time, Brian and I had watched three close family members die of cancer. I never envisioned that I could hurt so badly. The pain would have been unbearable if God hadn't encouraged me with faithful friends who showed their love and concern.

Mary Ann's short hospital visit didn't seem like much to her when she said, "I wish I could do something more to make this easier for you. " Didn't she know what a fresh face and loving words meant to one who had continually looked into faces etched with pain and the fear of dying?

"Let us know if there is anything we can do," implored Denise and Dayna as I got out of their car. Couldn't they see what a boost this day of shopping, lunch, and craft shows had been to my sagging spirits? And when Stephanie showed up at my door delivering warm lasagna, I wondered if she knew how much her home-cooked meal meant to us, who were longing for any food not served in a hospital cafeteria. How blessed I was to have friends who desperately wanted to ease my pain—and loved me enough to do it.

VICKEY BANKS

TAKING TIME FOR KINDNESS

When Clara's school took one hundred sixth-grade students to Washington, D. C., she went along as a sponsor. The last day as they toured the national aquarium, Brittney, a new student whom Clara knew only slightly, collapsed. Brittney felt alone and scared when she woke up in the ambulance, without her parents or anyone she knew. But soon after arriving at the ER, she saw Clara peek through the door into the room. Instead of going on with the group to lunch and more sightseeing, Clara had taken time to find Brittany at the hospital. Later Brittany said, "I'd never been in an emergency like that before. Your kindness mattered. You held my hand. You prayed with me. It was powerful. You were like my grandmother. I remember the peace I felt when you said, 'If we have to stay a few days longer while the other students return home, I'll stay with you because I'm your friend. I'm here for you.'"

A BOOMERANG BLESSING

Every Thursday for many years, my friend Cynthia headed across town to visit Maureen, a ninety year old woman who was crippled by arthritis. Cynthia took her out to lunch and ran errands each time she came. Yet the blessing of encouragement Cynthia gave to the elderly woman boomeranged right back to her own life—Cynthia knew few people in town and had no family around to share her pregnancy or the joy over her newborn child, so Maureen's interest and motherly wisdom were a special blessing. This "pocketful of time" shared between a younger woman and an older woman turned out to be a blessing for them both!

Be kind and gentle to those who are old for kindness is dearer and better than gold.

UNKNOWN

The boomerang power of giving happens in us at the very moment we enter the life of someone else in a positive, life-bringing way. Our spirit is lifted, our character is made stronger, our own path is straightened.

BARBARA JOHNSON

TIME FOR ROMANCE

One of the most thoughtful and creative gifts my husband and I ever received was "The Romance Fund." Some friends gave us a coupon stating that every month for the first year of our marriage, on the twenty-sixth day of the month (our wedding date), we would receive a check for $25 to use solely for a date together.

It is difficult to describe how much this gift meant to us. I had married a widower with three small children. We were missionaries in student ministry and therefore had no funds for such things as babysitters and dates. That "Romance Fund" check literally saved my life each month the first year of marriage. We could always look forward to TIME TOGETHER, which is certainly one of the best gifts anyone can give two people who are trying to form a newly married relationship amidst the demands of "instant" parenthood.

LUCINDA SECREST MCDOWELL

LISTENING FROM THE HEART

In order really to understand, we need to listen, not to reply. We need to listen long and attentively. In order to help anybody to open his heart, we have to give him time, asking only a few questions, as carefully as possible. . . . Above all we must not give the impression that we know better than he does what he must do. Otherwise we force him to withdraw.

PAUL TOURNIER

When my husband listens, it's with full attention. When I had a problem at the office he could see was troubling me, he turned off the TV, sat down and said, "Tell me about it." I talked and he listened. It was like confiding in a good friend I could really trust. To me, that's love—showing that you're each other's best friend.

PURI LACONICO

Take a moment to listen today
To what your children are trying to say
Listen today, whatever you do.

Listen to their problems
Listen for their needs.
Praise their smallest triumphs
Praise their smallest deeds.
Tolerate their chatter,
Amplify their laughter.
Find out what's the matter
Find out what they're after . . .

Take a moment to listen today
To what your children are trying to say,
Listen today, whatever you do
And they will come back to listen to you.

ANONYMOUS

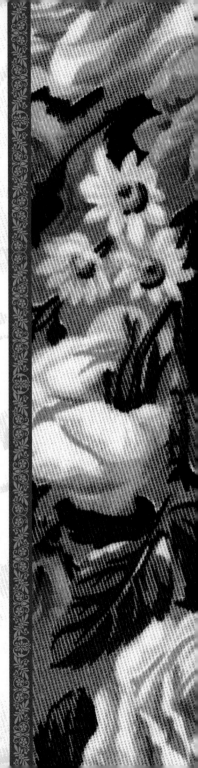

R emember to ask your kids more than you tell them. . . . Resolve to find out what your child is feeling or thinking, with no preconceived notions of a right or wrong answer. Ask what she would invent if given all the money in the world to develop it. Ask her about her wildest dreams. Ask her what she would be if she were a color, a wild animal, a member of the circus. Where would she go if she were a great adventurer?

BARBARA JOHNSON

Be slow to speak, quick to listen, and slow to anger.

JAMES 1:19

A LIFEBOAT OF LOVE

A teacher who listens and cares can be a lifeboat to a child who is "drowning" on the seas of life. A woman I once met told me her third-grade teacher was this kind of listener. During that time of her young life, the child was very frightened and alone. Her mom was a single parent who worked two jobs to support the family

*L*ove that cares, listens.

PAUL TILLICH

and was too exhausted at night to spend time listening to her daughter. During that year, the eight-year-old was being molested by a neighbor and family member, but she couldn't find a way to tell her mother.

"I didn't know how, but my teacher listened to me, encouraged me, and saw me as a real separate person. When she talked to me, she always got down on my eye level and really listened, something no other adult in my life ever did. That is something I've never forgotten . . . that at least once in my childhood, I mattered. "

GIVING A POCKETFUL OF TIME

➤ A standing date for Saturday morning breakfast at a nearby pancake house can be a perfect opportunity for mother and daughter, spouses or friends to talk and listen, connecting heart-to-heart.

➤ Take an inexpensive loaf of bread to a local lake and feed the ducks with your kids. Take a frisbee to throw or bubbles to blow and have a ball. Some of the best conversation often flows out of the most simple moments spent together.

➤ Tutor an at-risk child once a week who needs help with reading. The time you give will yield a harvest of benefits in what this child, with encouragement and help, achieves in the future.

Lonely people, hurting people need someone to help them up. To encourage them, to support them, to let them know they're not alone. Who are the helpers, the comforters for the times when we're bleeding and need a transfusion of love?

BILLY GRAHAM

Let's see how inventive we can be in encouraging love and helping out . . . spurring each other on, especially as we see the big Day approaching.

HEBREWS 10:25, THE MESSAGE

MY TIME IS YOURS

When Cyndi's husband Steve lay in a coma in ICU after being hit head-on by a drunk driver, the doctors told her he might not make it through the night. Earlier that day, friends and family had crowded in the emergency room and surgery waiting room, but now everyone had returned to their own homes for the night. So at 11:00 p. m., Cyndi paced the hall outside ICU and faced a long, lonely night.

Suddenly, she looked up and saw Debbie—loaded with pillows, blankets, and sandwiches—bound through the heavy doors. Although Debbie's children were hosting their first-ever sleepover at her house, Debbie had left the festivities to join Cyndi in her hospital vigil.

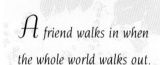

A friend walks in when the whole world walks out.

WALTER
WINCHELL

"I'm here to wait out the night with you. My time is yours," Debbie whispered, hugging her friend around the neck. A huge wave of relief rushed over Cyndi, sweeping away the nagging anxiety about being alone all night. Debbie's presence gave Cyndi the courage to get through one of the hardest nights of her life.

*Friends are angels who lift our
feet when our own wings have
trouble remembering how to fly.*

UNKNOWN

*It takes no special talent,
Makes no difference who you are,
To light a little candle
That outshines the brightest star.*

*It doesn't call for sacrifice
To provide a little light
That might be the ray of hope
For someone through the night.*

CLARENCE BERTRAM DENNISON

Sometimes in life a warm embrace goes even farther than words to encourage the heart. Taking time to physically demonstrate love or caring can make a world of difference, infuse confidence and hope in people— no matter what their age or stage of life.

Hugs go together with heartprints. Whatever you do that is compassionate, kind, comforting, or affectionate is a heartprint. Even if it's isn't Valentine's Day, a smackaroo on the cheek might do a loved one good. An arm around someone's shoulder. A firm handshake. A kiss on the tips of the toes. A hand to hold. A full body squeeze. A tear dried with your fingertips. A playful tickle.

BARBARA JOHNSON

GIVE A HUG

It's wondrous what a hug can do.
A hug can cheer you when you're blue.
A hug can say, "I love you so"
Or "Gee! I hate to see you go. "
A hug is "Welcome back again!" and
"Great to see you!" or "Where've you been?"
A hug can soothe a small child's pain
And bring a rainbow after rain.
The hug! There's just no doubt about it,
We scarcely could survive without it.
A hug delights and warms and charms,
It must be why God gave us arms.
Hugs are great for fathers and mothers,
Sweet for sisters, swell for brothers.
Chances are some favorite aunts,
Love them more than potted plants.
Kittens crave them, puppies love them
Heads of state are not above them.
A hug can break the language barrier
And make the dullest day seem merrier.
No need to fret about the store of 'em,
The more you give the more there are of 'em.
So stretch those arms without delay and
Give someone a hug today!

ANONYMOUS

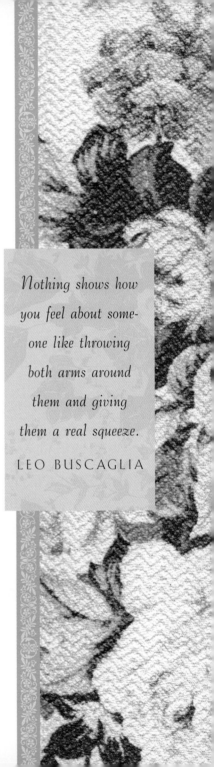

Nothing shows how you feel about some-one like throwing both arms around them and giving them a real squeeze.

LEO BUSCAGLIA

SUNDAY MORNING HUGS

One of my sweetest memories is of Jay, our child with Down syndrome, attending worship service as a toddler. Every Sunday morning, he would run to our pastor after the service ended. The pastor would scoop him up in his arms, give him a big hug, and hold him while shaking hands with all the church members. I offered more than once to take Jay, but the pastor refused. In embracing Jay, he also allowed the church members to meet and love this little toddler with special needs in a unique way. These Sunday morning hugs helped Jay feel as if he "belonged" to the whole church and made him know it was true what the pastor said in his sermons—Jesus did love him!

LOUISE TUCKER JONES

Where there is great love,
there are always miracles.

UNKNOWN

Real giving has its joy in
imagining the joy of the receiver.
It means choosing, expending time,
going out of one's way.

THEODOR W. ADORNO

A TIME TO SMILE

Give the gift of a smile to those you meet, work with, and love today. Our faces, which contain either approval or disapproval, dislike or love, mirror to others what they are becoming. Our faces encourage or discourage. Let your looks of encouragement build up and spark hope in those you see today.

The best way to cheer yourself is to

try to cheer somebody else up.

MARK TWAIN

THE GIFT OF A SMILE

As teachers we can easily think that our instruction is the best thing we offer our students. But the day I received this letter, I realized that it's the little things—like the way we look at students—that lift their hearts: "Dear Mrs. Fuller, I really appreciate your coming. I hope you like our classroom! You have taught me so many things about writing, but what I love is the way that you always walk in our class with a smile on your face. Thank you so much! From Sara Hawkins."

It was only a sunny smile,
and little it cost in the giving.
But like the morning light, it scattered the night,
and made the day worth living.

ANONYMOUS

MOTHER'S GIFT TO ME

When Heather Whitestone lost most of her hearing at eighteen months of age, the doctor told her mother that the little girl would probably never learn to speak or go beyond third grade. But her mom patiently encouraged her during the six long years it took Heather to learn to say her last name correctly. Mrs. Whitestone enrolled Heather in a clinic that advocated ocoupedics—learning to listen and speak rather than using sign language—and took her to dance classes where Heather fell in love with ballet. Years later she achieved what many said was impossible—she became Miss America 1995.

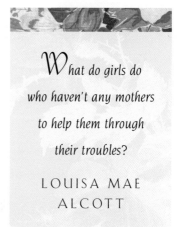

What do girls do who haven't any mothers to help them through their troubles?

LOUISA MAE ALCOTT

Heather attributes her success to her mom's encouragement: "One of my biggest blessings has been my mother, who looks at me as a person with a heart, not a disability," she says.

A CHANCE TO LAUGH AND DANCE

*M*onica's cancer was back with a vengeance, and that frail ten-year-old was the saddest child to watch as she pulled an IV pole around the clinic at Children's Hospital. In just ten short years, Monica had suffered more pain than most of us experience in a lifetime. One of her legs had been amputated, and although she was fighting valiantly, she was losing her battle with cancer. That's what made the party Kay and Marsha gave for her so special.

The memories we collect and give brighten our lives as long as we live.

JULIE SNEYD

As I entered the art center, fifties music blared from a boom box. Dressed up in a poodle skirt with a scarf around her neck, Monica was serving root beer floats to other children from the clinic. A smile lit up her face. This party was a gift of time, carefully planned by volunteers to lift Monica's spirits.

It was just a pocketful of time—but it gave her a chance to laugh, to dance the twist and, for a short while, to feel like a normal kid again.

GIFT-OF-TIME COUPONS

*f*or birthday or Christmas, each family member can give coupons to the others with a promised service (like cleaning, breakfast in bed, gardening help) or time spent together (like a day at the zoo with Dad, or a camping trip). The coupon might read, "This coupon entitles you to a special breakfast in bed any Saturday of your choice in the month of February. Love, Alison." Write the promise on a blank index card, put it in a bright envelope, and hang it on Christmas tree or beside a birthday person's dinner plate.

1. Do something in addition to your own job description, especially if someone else is running behind. For example, make your own copies, team up with a fellow employee to help him or her meet a deadline, or fetch specialty coffee drinks for everyone on your team or in your department.

2. If you hear of a local disaster, offer to help those affected rebuild their lives. If you have the resources, go to the location of a national or worldwide disaster and help however you can.

3. Take an hour to honor God's creativity: Watch a sunset (or a sunrise if you're an early riser); take a walk and admire the trees, wildflowers, and wildlife; watch the clouds float by; or during a storm, stop what you're doing and drink in God's power as He expresses it.

4. Offer to be a taxi driver for your neighbor's kids.

5. Invite your children to participate in a creative activity you can usually do by yourself much more quickly, such as baking cookies or arranging flowers. If you don't have kids of your own, invite kids from the neighborhood to join you.

6. Invite someone to dinner whose spouse, family, or roommate is out of town.

7. Think of someone who needs to know the Lord. Pick a time of day that symbolizes that person (for example, if his or her birthday is August 5, choose 8:05). Whenever you look at a clock and it's that time of day, pray for that person's salvation.

8. Offer to be a church volunteer substitute—make it known that you'll substitute for Sunday school teachers who need a break.

9. Look service people—waiters, store clerks, grocery baggers—in the eye when they help you. Take the time to ask them how they're doing and authentically converse with them. Patiently wait when they take longer to serve you than you'd like.

10. Be willing to take longer to drive to a destination—let other drivers in ahead of you when you can.

11. Let the answering machine get your phone calls when you're eating dinner or entertaining a friend—make those times sacred by coming to them with your undivided attention.

12. Remain positive when your spouse has to stay late at work occasionally—he would rather be home too!

LISA LAUFFER

THE GIFT OF ONE'S SELF

I was sitting in bed the day before Christmas with a broken right arm and elbow, surrounded by gifts that hadn't been wrapped, a "To-Do" list I would never get done, and a house that desperately needed cleaning since family members were coming for Christmas and our son's wedding. I'd been up most of the night in pain. The day was overcast and gloomy, but my heart was even gloomier. How was I going to make even the most basic preparations for Christmas?

Suddenly, the telephone rang. "We're on our way over, so make a list of what you need done and we'll do it!" Susan said from her car phone. In a short while she and Marilyn, friends from our House Church, arrived and swooped in like Mr. Clean, putting things in order, vacuuming, dusting, and cleaning the kitchen. "What's next?" they asked when that was done. I pointed at the pile of unwrapped gifts.

Encouragement is oxygen to the soul.

GEORGE M. ADAMS

Just then Connie walked in and joined them in wrapping presents and fashioning lovely bows to adorn them. When all the work was complete, we brewed a pot of Christmas tea, brought out a tin of cookies, and sat by the fire chatting and reading Christmas stories aloud. Their gift of time had encouraged my heart beyond words. These dear friends had certainly shown to me that the best gift is truly the gift of one's self.

ACKNOWLEDGMENTS

*Grateful acknowledgment is made to the following
publishers for permission to reprint copyrighted material.*

Brestin, Dee. *Friendships of Women*. Wheaton: Victor books,
©1988 Cook communications Ministries. Used by permission. May not be further reproduced. All rights reserved.

Gordon, Arthur, *A Touch of Wonder*. Grand Rapids: Fleming
Revell, 1974, a division of Baker Book House Company.

Johnson, Barbara. *Boomerang Joy*. Grand Rapids: Zondervan,
©1998 by Barbara Johnson. Used by permission of
Zondervan Publishing House.

Tylka, Barbara L., *Country Living*, June, 1995. Reprinted
by permission of Country Living, ©1995 by the Hearst
Corporation.